INSECTS

Joyce Pope

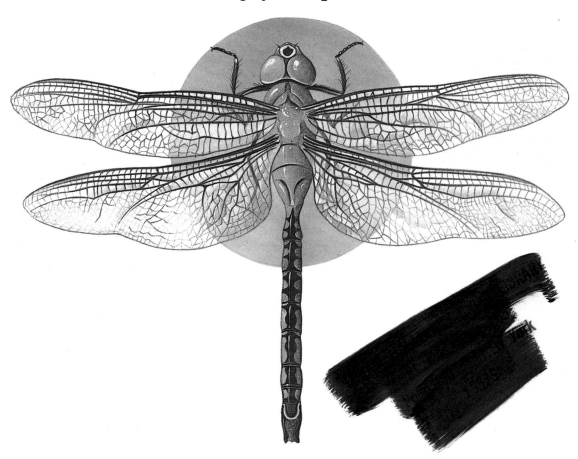

Franklin Watts

London   New York   Toronto   Sydney

© 1984 Franklin Watts Ltd

First published in Great
Britain in 1984
by Franklin Watts Ltd
12a Golden Square
London W1

First published in the United
States of America by
Franklin Watts Inc.
387 Park Avenue South
New York
N.Y. 10016

Phototypeset by Tradespools
Ltd, Frome, Somerset
Printed in Italy

UK edition:
ISBN 0 86313 182 4
US edition:
ISBN 0-531-03815-7
Library of Congress
Catalog Card Number:
84-51177

Designed by
Ben White

Illustrated by
Colin Newman, Val Sangster/
Linden Artists, and Chris
Forsey

INSECTS

Contents

Equipment

As well as a few everyday items, you will need the following equipment to carry out the activities in this book.

Bamboo cane	Paintbrush
Blotting paper	Pencils
Clear acetate sheet	Penknife
Cookie tin	Pieces of cut fruit
Detergent	Plastic boxes
Elastic bands	Plastic tubes
Enamel plate	Ruler
Flour	Sand
Graph paper	Scotch tape
Hand lens	Spiral bound notebook
Jam jars	Strong garden wire
Needle	Sugar
Old net curtains	Tape measure

Introduction

We human beings think that we are very important—as indeed we are. But human beings like us have lived only about 40,000 years. This means that as far as the earth is concerned we are newcomers. Insects have existed for 400 million years. Today at least a million different kinds of insects are already known and scientists are finding new ones every week.

There are more insects than any other sort of animal. They live almost everywhere on earth except where it is very cold all through the year. Some live in forests, some in grassy places, others live in lakes or rivers, on mountains or in deserts. A few even live in the sea. Some kinds of insects are found in huge numbers. For example, there may be more locusts in a single swarm than there are people living on earth.

Some insects live in our homes or eat our food, so we call them pests. But most insects have little to do with us and they usually eat things that we do not want. They are an important part of our world. Some eat dead plants and animals, which pass through their bodies and into the soil. This means that plants may once more use the minerals from which they were made. Other insects are important because they carry pollen from flower to flower. Without insects, the earth would be a poorer and much less beautiful place. Finding out about insects helps us to understand the world in which we live.

What is an insect?

A bee is an insect. A beetle is an insect. A fly is an insect. This gives us a clue to one of the most important things about insects, which is that most of them can fly. But so can birds, and bats, so how are insects different?

The main difference is that insects are animals without backbones. They are supported and protected from outside by armor made of chitin. This is a bit like the material our fingernails are made of. Only very small creatures can be made in this way. The heaviest insects weigh only about $3\frac{1}{2}$ oz (100 grams).

△Many insects live on the ground, hiding among fallen leaves. Turn these over and you may find tiny springtails and ants feeding. You may also find beetles, such as the dark-colored, fast-moving hunters called ground beetles.

△No matter where you live, you can find insects around you. Look on a sun-warmed wall and you will probably see small flies resting. They are easily frightened because they have many enemies, including spiders, birds and human beings.

△Some insects hide under stones and logs. You may find an earwig tending her eggs in such a place. Or you could find beetles. Remember to replace anything that you move so that the animals you are studying are not disturbed for long.

▷When you collect insects, you should put each one into a separate container. When you get home, you can sort out your collection. If the insects are moving too fast, put the containers into a very cool place and this will slow the insects down. Then you can examine them before releasing them.

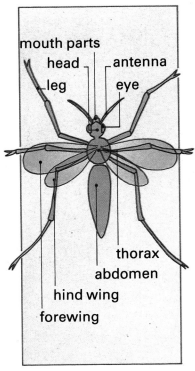

△Insects' bodies are always built in three parts: the head, which has the antennae or feelers on it; the thorax, which has one or two pairs of wings but never more than three pairs of legs; and the abdomen, which has no legs or wings.

Some insects, such as caterpillars and ants do not have wings. This is because only adult insects can fly and a caterpillar is the young stage of a butterfly or moth. Ants live much of their lives under ground, where wings would not be of much use.

So how can you tell if a creature without wings is an insect? The name insect should give you a clue because you can see that an insect's body is made *in sect*ions. There are three main sections. Each section has a different job to do.

The first is the head, where you can see the eyes and feelers, and the mouth. But insects do not have noses. The second part is called the thorax. This has three pairs of jointed legs and usually two pairs of wings. The third part is called the abdomen. This contains the main digestive organs, the sex organs, the fat reserves and the breathing pores.

7

Sorting insects

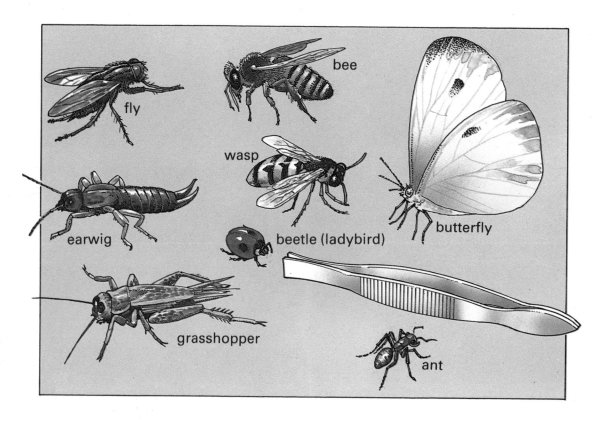

One of the things that you will soon discover when you start to look at insects is that there are many different kinds. Sometimes you may find a dead insect. You can examine it more closely with a hand lens. You should always handle insects with great care because their bodies are very fragile and they are easily damaged.

You will notice that most sorts of insects have two pairs of wings. They flap these together because it is more efficient to use them in this way. Some insects, like ladybird beetles and earwigs keep their back wings hidden, while others, like the ant, do not have any.

△ This picture shows you some of the different sorts of insects that you may find. Although they vary in shape and color, you can see that they are all insects, because each one has a head, a thorax and an abdomen. Most of them have wings as well.

Is it an insect?

While you are searching for insects, you will find lots of other small creatures. How will you be able to know whether you have found an insect or not? The first thing to remember is that only insects have wings. But in case you have found a wingless insect, see if its body is in three sections. If it is not, you may have found a snail or a slug. These creatures have only one big slab of muscle and they are not insects.

Centipedes, millipedes, spiders and woodlice are made in sections—in fact they are related to insects—but the sections are arranged differently. They also have more than six legs. Spiders are probably the creatures that are most easily confused with insects. But you can tell them apart if you remember that insects always have three parts to their bodies and six legs. Spiders have only two sections to their bodies and they have eight legs.

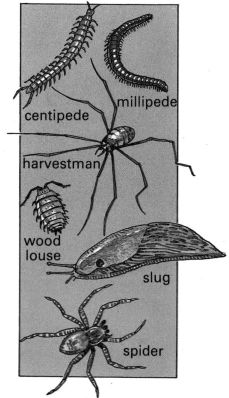

△These are some common animals without backbones which are not insects.

▷Put the insect that you want to draw on a piece of graph paper. Using a sharp pencil, make marks on the paper at the top of the insect's head, the tip of its abdomen and the ends of its wings. Then make more marks around it. Eventually you will have enough marks to join them up and make a diagram.

Remember to record the date and where you found the insect on each drawing. Try to identify the type of insect.

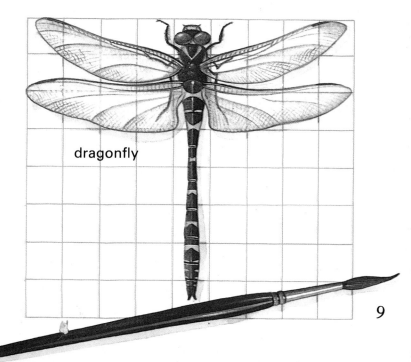

dragonfly

9

Life cycles

Like human beings, insects are small when they are young and grow until they are adults. But, unlike us, they grow in stages. Very few insects care for their young after they have hatched. Instead, they lay their eggs in places where the young will find food easily. In some insects, the hatchlings look like small versions of their parents. As they feed, they grow, but their skeleton-like armor does not grow with them. Eventually it splits and is shed. Underneath there is a new, soft skin which can stretch for a short time, but it soon hardens to become a new suit of armor. After each molt, the young become more like their parents. In most cases, when they have shed their skin for the last time, they are able to fly.

▽ Caterpillars chew the leaves of plants with their horny jaws. They spend most of their time eating. But because they are slow-moving and helpless, they must be protected against such enemies as birds. Some caterpillars are difficult to see and some taste so bad that nothing wants to eat them. When a caterpillar is full-grown, it turns into a chrysalis, which lies hidden on the ground, or among the leaves.

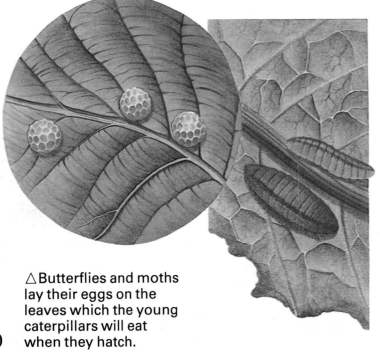

△ Butterflies and moths lay their eggs on the leaves which the young caterpillars will eat when they hatch.

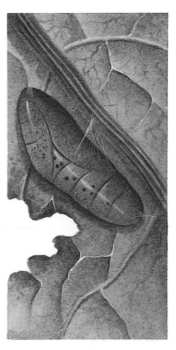

△In the chrysalis, the body of the caterpillar changes to become a butterfly or moth. When the change is complete, the case opens and the adult insect emerges. At first its wings are soft and crumpled, but the insect pumps air into its veins. The wings spread and harden and it can fly.

In many sorts of insects, the young that hatch from the eggs look nothing whatever like their parents. They look more like worms, or like centipedes with too few legs. These creatures are called larvae. They must feed and grow as quickly as they can. Larvae are not usually able to see much, or to move fast. They avoid their enemies by living in hidden places, or by tasting so nasty that nothing will attack them.

When the larvae have eaten all they need, they find a safe place where they change into the adult form by a process called pupation.

During pupation the insect is quite still, but it is not resting. Inside the chrysalis or pupa case, its body is being rearranged to make the adult shape. The adult finally emerges from the pupa and can fly. It must then find a mate so that females can lay eggs to make new generations of insects.

▷The adult butterfly sucks nectar from flowers, because it does not need to feed as it searches for a mate. Its life will not be long, once it has mated or laid eggs.

Feeding

◁Sugar crystals in a jar may attract flies. Because they cannot chew the sugar, they spit on it to dissolve it.

▷A piece of cut fruit will be visited by lots of insects. Some will suck up the juice and others will chew at the soft pulp.

Insects have to eat, just like all animals but they eat very little. Most of them will eat only one thing and will starve to death if that is not available. It sounds very dull to us. Imagine being a caterpillar and feeding on the leaves of only one sort of plant. Count up all of the different things you have eaten in a single day and you will soon see the difference.

Mouth parts

The very first insects were probably scavengers, feeding on dead animals and plant remains. Today, some insects still chew away with mouth parts much like those of their ancient ancestors. But insect jaws are very different from our own jaws. They do not have upper and lower jaws as we do. Instead, they have a pair of biting mandibles that work from side to side, to cut and crush food. Below these, a second pair of jaw parts, called maxillae, help to pull chopped up bits of food into the mouth. The maxillae often have long,

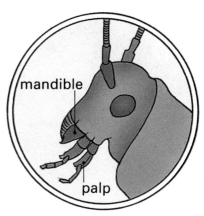

△The mouth parts of a grasshopper look very complicated. The hard jaws or mandibles do the main job of chewing while the long palps touch and taste the food. Many sorts of insects that feed on tough things like leaves have similar mouth parts.

ant trail to food

△If you put some sugar a few feet from an ants' nest, the insects will soon find the food.

The first ant to do so will take some back to the nest. Soon lots of ants will come to take the sugar. They find their way by following their own scent trails. If you wipe your finger across the track they are using, the ants will be confused by the strange scent.

finger-like palps at the side. These touch the food and make quite sure that it is suitable for the insect to eat. Above the mandibles there is a horny upper lip called the labrum. Below the maxillae there is a lower lip, or labium.

Insects with biting mouth parts, such as cockroaches, grasshoppers and beetles, often feed on the same sort of food all through their lives. Other insects do most or all of their feeding in the grub, or larva stage. Once they are adult, they do not need to grow and some adult insects eat nothing at all. With others, a little sugary food gives them enough energy. In these insects the mouth parts have become altered to form a tube through which they can feed. They drink the juices of plants.

13

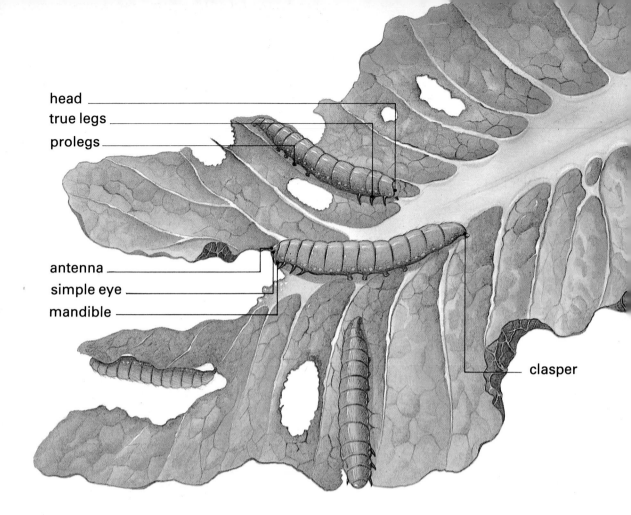

head

true legs

prolegs

antenna

simple eye

mandible

clasper

How a caterpillar eats

If you are out for a walk in the summer, you can often find a group of caterpillars on the leaves of plants. They may not look like insects because they seem to have too many legs. But only the three pairs behind the head are true legs. The others are called "prolegs" and are there largely to support the long hind end of the body.

If you listen, you can often hear the champing noise made by a caterpillar's tiny jaws as it feeds. The caterpillar's body is just a bag for food. It spends most of its time eating. Because of this, beneath oak trees in springtime, the ground is often black with caterpillar droppings.

△ The caterpillar or larval stage is the time when an insect grows. It hatches on its food supply and immediately starts eating. The caterpillar has poor senses, so it knows little about anything beyond the leaf it feeds on.

Flesh-eating insects

Not all insects eat plants. Many feed on the flesh of other creatures, often of other insects. Flesh-eating insects are very useful to farmers and gardeners because they destroy lots of pests. Ladybird beetles are so useful to farmers and fruit-growers that they are often put among the crops to destroy pests such as greenflies.

In the early stages of their lives, the grubs of wasps and hornets are fed on flesh. Adult wasps can often be seen hunting for food for the young of their colony. Strangely, they also seem to like salty things and can sometimes be seen using their powerful mandibles to cut a circle out of a piece of ham or smoked fish.

Some flesh-eating beetles hunt caterpillars, while others feed on snails, often killing and eating animals many times their own size. In some places, these beetles are protected by law.

△Flesh-eating insects usually feed on other insects. A few, like hornets, may sometimes help themselves to our food, but as a rule they find plenty to feed their grubs on in the wild.

△Although many ants feed on other insects, they do not usually eat aphids. Instead they protect them. Aphids produce a sweet substance called honeydew. The ants "milk" the aphids for it.

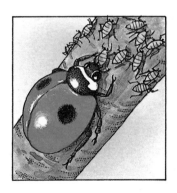

△Most ladybird beetles feed on aphids and other pests. During its life, a single ladybird beetle may eat 600 aphids. Farmers often encourage them by putting out boxes for them to hibernate in.

15

Energy from sugar

Adult insects do not grow, or replace tissues, so they need very little food. Many insects get the energy for flight by feeding on nectar in the same way as cyclists often drink glucose, a form of sugar. Nectar is a sugary fluid made by flowers. Insects that feed on nectar include bees, butterflies, moths, flies, wasps and beetles.

Nectar is formed on flower petals in tiny cups, called nectaries. Sometimes these lie near the top of the flowers. Beetles and flies can sip the nectar from the open cups.

In some flowers, however, the nectar is hidden deep inside the petals and only insects with long tongues can reach it. Their tongues are usually formed by the mandibles or maxillae becoming deeply grooved. When they are pressed together they make a tube. This is like a built-in drinking straw, through which the nectar can be sucked.

▽ The mouth parts of a bee have become tube-like and are called a proboscis. The proboscis is rigid and not very long, but it enables the bee to suck up nectar that is deep inside flowers.

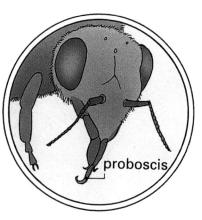

proboscis

▷ Flowers are generally brilliantly colored to attract insects to the center of the blossom where the nectar is hidden. In its search for sweet food, the insect gets pollen on its body and carries it to other flowers. Some of the pollen will get dusted onto the flowers that the insect visits. This fertilizes the flowers and seeds develop. Most pollinating insects have hairy bodies, so that pollen sticks easily.

Bees have fairly short tube-mouths. Bumble bees have longer tubes than honey bees, so they can feed on nectar that is more deeply hidden. Honey bees sometimes get over the problem of not being able to reach the nectar by biting a hole in the base of the flower to take it. This means that they do not pollinate the flower when searching for the nectar.

Butterflies and moths have the longest tongues of all. In some tropical species they may be over 10 in (25 cm) long and can reach food at the ends of the long, tube-like flowers of some orchids. Butterfly and moth tongues are so long that when the insects are not feeding they are curled up out of the way, under the insect's head.

A few flies have long tongues, but these are never curled. Look for the bee-fly in the early summer. It carries its tongue ahead of it like a lance.

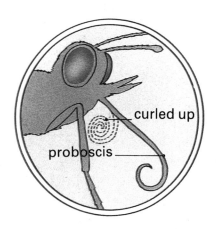

curled up

proboscis

△Butterflies and moths have very long tongues. They curl up out of the way when the insect is not feeding.

▷You can make an insect garden by growing food for insects and their grubs.

Scented flowers such as lavender attract bees. Heavily scented blooms like honeysuckle and Buddleia (butterfly bush) are right for long-tongued moths and butterflies. In the spring, primroses, wallflowers and lilacs attract insects such as the bee-fly. Nettles are the food of many caterpillars.

Watching insects

As soon as you start watching insects, you will discover that there are lots of things that they can do. Many of them are the same things that you do, like breathing and eating, or exploring their world by sight, smell and touch. But insects do most of these things in a different way from us.

Insects must breathe in oxygen, but they do not have noses. Instead, they have a line of breathing holes down the sides of their bodies. You can see these most easily on a caterpillar, although almost all insects have them.

Most insects can see and recognize color. They can smell and taste food too. Some butterflies have taste organs on their feet. Very few insects hear in the same way as we can. Those that do have "ears" on their sides or, like bush crickets, on their front knees.

▷Looper caterpillars are sometimes called "inchworms" because of the way that they move. They have to hitch themselves forward until their bodies are humped up into a tall loop. Then, gripping with their back ends, they extend their front ends until they are flat again. Looper caterpillars eventually turn into moths. If you find one, measure the length of its "stride" and see if the name "inchworm" is a good one.

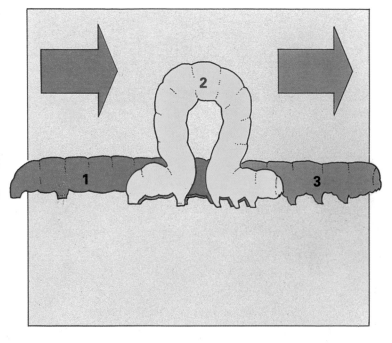

▽You can sometimes find tiny footprints made by insects in sand or very soft mud. To see how they make the footprints, sift some flour on to an old plate and put some different insects on it.

▽In the diagram, the red legs always move forward at the same time, while the blue legs remain on the ground. Then the blue legs move forward. Look at the footprints on your floured plate. You will be able to see how the pattern is formed by this method of moving the legs. You may need a hand lens.

How insects walk

Land insects walk in a different way from people. They often go so fast that it is difficult to see how they are using their legs. If you could slow an insect down, you would see that it always moves two legs on one side of its body forward at the same time as it moves one leg on the other side. This means that its body is always supported by three legs. Some long-bodied insects have extra support towards the back of the abdomen. Caterpillars, for example, have extra legs called pro-legs or false legs.

Some insects can move over very smooth surfaces. If you could examine their feet under a high-powered microscope, you would see that they have thousands of very tiny hairs, which act together like suckers. This is why a ladybird beetle can walk up a window or a fly can stay on the ceiling.

19

△A ladybird beetle has to unpack its wings from beneath its elytra. It is hard to get them back in place. You often see ladybird beetles trailing their wings.

△The wings of moths and butterflies are gauzy and transparent, but they are covered with thousands of tiny scales which give them their colors.

△Lacewings have four large wings with a fine net of veins. Usually, insects that have a grub or caterpillar stage to their lives have fewer veins in their wings.

Wings and flight

Insects move best by flying. It enables them to go quickly from place to place, to find food or a mate, and to escape from enemies. Many insects have two pairs of wings. Some, such as dragonflies, use them separately and you can hear them rattle against each other as they fly.

Most insects, however, use the two wings on each side of the body together, so that they do not clash. Butterflies and moths have fore and hind wings that overlap. As one wing goes up and down it automatically carries the other with it. Bees and wasps have wings linked together by a series of hooks. Flies use only the forewings for flight. The hind wings have become very tiny and are used to help with balance. Beetles fly using their gauzy hind wings. These are normally folded away under the hardened forewings (elytra), used in flight to give "lift."

△Most insects fly best in the sunshine. This is because they are cold-blooded animals and cannot be active at low temperatures. A few fly at night, when the weather is cooler. In this picture, moths are attracted by a bright lamp.

Insects beat their wings very fast when they fly. This beating of the wings in the air makes a buzzing sound. The higher the pitch of the sound, the faster the wings are moving. A bee, which makes a fairly low-pitched sound, is beating its wings about 250 times a second. Some small flies beat their wings over 1000 times a second, making a high-pitched whine. Most insects do not fly very great distances, but some are able to travel over thousands of miles.

Although they can fly, grasshoppers and their relatives escape from danger by jumping. To show just how far a grasshopper can jump, catch one on a summer's day and put it carefully on the end of a ruler or tape measure. It will probably jump as soon as you remove your hand.

Try catching different sorts of grasshoppers to see which can jump the furthest.

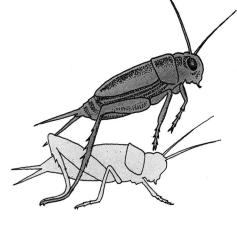

△Grasshoppers and their relatives can leap away from danger, using huge, strongly muscled hind legs. They can often fly as well. Look at an insect's wings. They are supported and strengthened by struts called veins. But their veins do not have blood in them as ours do.

Water insects

Many insects live in wet places. Some live in ponds or streams when they are young and come to dry land when they are adult. Many spend their whole lives in the water. Some insects live below the surface of the water, but others are supported on top.

Pond skaters carry a tiny cushion of air on their feet so they do not break the surface. To see how this works, take a jar of water. Put a needle on a piece of blotting paper and float the paper on the water. The blotting paper will sink to the bottom leaving the needle resting on the water. The water is strong enough to hold it on top.

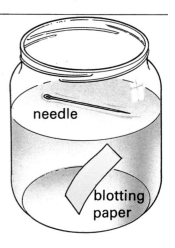

needle

blotting paper

△ You can break the strength of the water surface by putting a drop of detergent near the needle.

▷ If you stand and watch by a pond or stream you will see lots of different insects. Some, like midges, mayflies and dragonflies, fly about over the water looking for mates or food. Others, like pond skaters, water scorpions and whirligig beetles live on the surface of the water.

waterboatmen

backswimmer

water beetle

▷You can explore below the surface of a pond using a net. Take a double thickness of net and stitch it to a loop of strong wire. Push the ends of the wire into a garden cane. You may catch water beetles, backswimmers and water boatmen.

Watch them carefully and make a note of the different ways in which they move. Then put them carefully back into the water.

Swimmers and divers

Below the surface of a pond or stream you can find insects living in much the same way as those on land. Some are scavengers, some are plant feeders and some are hunters.

Insects that can swim usually have flattened, oar-like legs, often fringed with hairs. Among the fiercest hunters are dragonfly nymphs. They attack other insects, tadpoles and even small fish. They trap their prey from a safe distance, shooting out their sharp, curved mandibles on an arm called a mask.

Water boatmen and backswimmers are also hunters. So is the great diving beetle, which attacks creatures far larger than itself.

Insects that live in water have special ways of getting oxygen for breathing. Some have gills so they can obtain it directly from the water. The diving beetle pushes the end of its abdomen above the water and traps a bubble of air beneath its wing cases, so that it can breathe while submerged.

23

Pond dipping

One of the best places to find insects in summer is in water. The insects you will find in ponds will be different from those that are found in streams, but they are quite easy to fish out with a net.

Icecream boxes make good tanks to examine your catch in because the insects show up well against the white plastic. When you have looked at them, put them back carefully into the water.

When you are looking at insects, remember that you are probably disturbing their homes. Try to be as careful as possible.

▽There are always new things to see when you are pond dipping. Dip the net deeply in the water as well as on the surface. You will find that different sorts of insects live at different depths. Keep a record of everything you find in your notebook, but remember to use a pencil or waterproof pen in case the book gets wet.

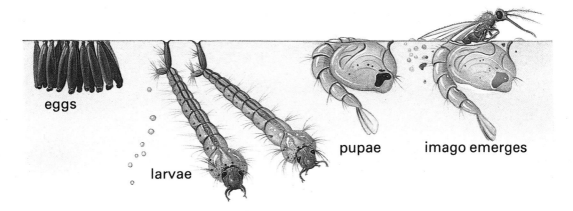

eggs

larvae

pupae

imago emerges

Keeping water insects

If you turn over stones at the edge of a stream, remember to turn them back again. Try not to disturb waterside plants, because they are shelter for many creatures.

One of the best ways to find out about water insects is to take them home. Make sure you have a tank prepared for them, so that they can go straight into their new living space. Do not take too many insects because it is easy to overcrowd a small tank, and also it is much easier to see what a few animals are doing. Remember to keep the hunters separate, or you will find yourself with a well-fed dragonfly nymph or diving beetle, and nothing else.

△ Look for the tiny rafts of floating mosquito eggs. These hatch into larvae which hang from the surface film of the water, pushing tiny snorkles into the air to breathe.

The pupa, from which the adult hatches, hangs just below the surface as well.

▽ Put each different sort of insect into a different jar, or they may eat each other.

You can watch how dragonfly nymphs feed by hanging a tiny piece of raw meat in the water. Do not leave it there too long or it will poison the water. Caddis fly larvae in their cases feed on water plants.

dragonfly nymph

meat on string

caddisfly larvae in cases

25

Keeping insects

You can learn a lot about insects by watching them in the garden or park, but one of the best ways to study insects is to keep them. Beetles and earwigs can be kept in icecream boxes or large coffee jars. They like to have some cover, so put some soil or sand and a piece of dead wood in the bottom. You can feed them on pieces of cut apple, but experiment with what they will eat by giving them tiny pieces of meat, cheese or bread. Do not leave any food in the box for more than a few hours, or it will go bad.

You should not try to keep butterflies, or any other insect that flies freely, because they will probably damage themselves on the cage walls. You can sometimes find the eggs of moths or butterflies. Keep these to rear and release them when they are adults and ready to fly.

▽ Plant-eating insects are easier to keep than flesh-eaters. You will find that most of them feed on common wild plants, or on weeds, like this nettle. They must have plenty of fresh leaves because they cannot eat wilted food.

▷ One method of being sure that your insects always have plenty of food is called "sleeving." Fold a piece of old net curtain and stitch it to make a bag. Place the bag over a leafy twig where insects such as caterpillars are feeding. Tie up the end with string so that they cannot escape and their enemies cannot get in. Move the insects and sleeve them to a new twig as the leaves get eaten.

You can buy eggs or caterpillars from a butterfly farm, but make sure that you can get the right food for them, or they will not survive. They will need a supply of leaves to eat. Push the stems of the plants into damp sand, or cover the mouth of the water jar in which you place them. If you do not do this, the insects may walk down into the water and drown.

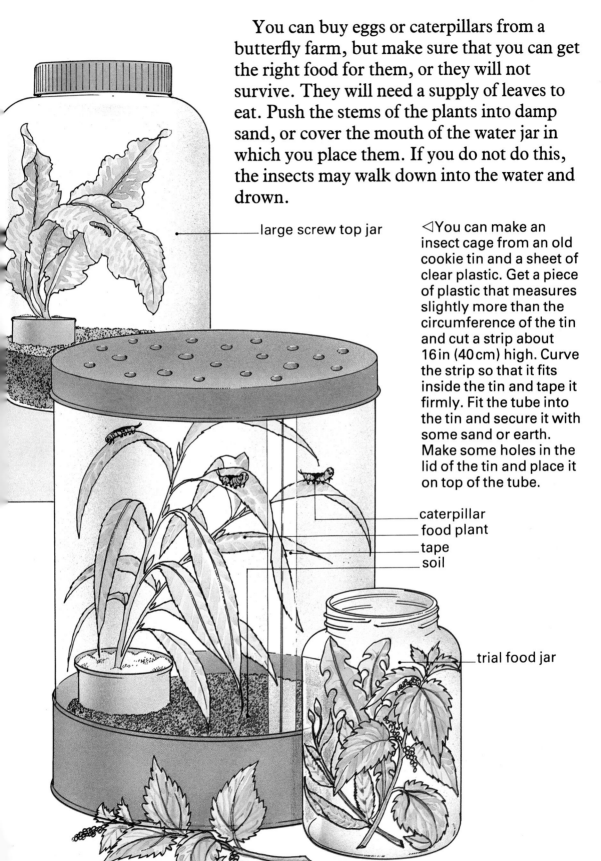

large screw top jar

◁You can make an insect cage from an old cookie tin and a sheet of clear plastic. Get a piece of plastic that measures slightly more than the circumference of the tin and cut a strip about 16 in (40 cm) high. Curve the strip so that it fits inside the tin and tape it firmly. Fit the tube into the tin and secure it with some sand or earth. Make some holes in the lid of the tin and place it on top of the tube.

caterpillar
food plant
tape
soil

trial food jar

27

Insect pets

When you keep insects it is easy to study their way of life.

You can discover things about your insects' feeding patterns. Study them when they are eating to find out whether they feed during the night or in the daytime. Make a note of whether they feed continuously for long periods. Do they avoid light, or do they enjoy it? You can try giving them different sorts of food to see which they prefer.

If you have a tape recorder, it is easy to do experiments to discover whether insects can hear sounds. With some insects you can try to find out whether they can see colors, and if so, which ones. Be very careful when handling your insects. Then none of these experiments should be in any way harmful to them.

△ Stick insects make good pets. Like most insects, they take up very little space, they do not smell and they are quiet. When you have kept laboratory stick insects successfully, you can try some of the larger kinds, which can sometimes be found in pet shops.

You should return any wild insects to the place where you found them after you have kept them for a few days.

If you want to keep an insect pet for a long time, the laboratory stick insect is one of the best to try. Almost all of these animals are females. Although they do not mate, they lay eggs which hatch into more females, so you may develop a colony of them. You should not let them get overcrowded. Stick insects are easy to feed because they eat privet or ivy leaves, which are easy to obtain almost anywhere. You should keep them in a warm place.

You can learn a great deal from your stick insect pets. Some of the things they do will help you to understand the lives of other insects.

▽ Many insects are camouflaged so that they can hide from their enemies. Some look like leaves, some like the bark of trees. Others can change their color to match their background. Try putting some light-colored stick insects on dark leaves like ivy. You will find that in two or three days, they have changed their color to match that of the leaves. Keep a "control" of light insects on light-colored leaves. They will not change color.

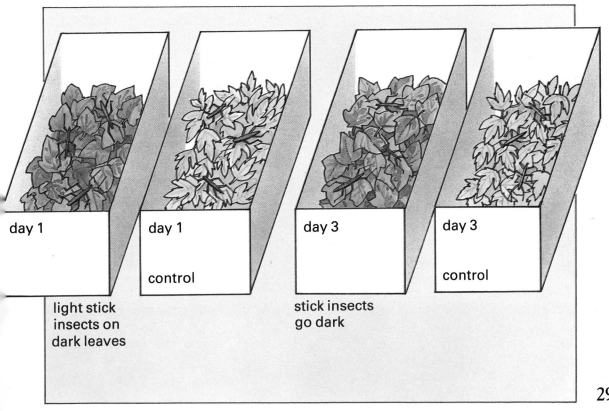

day 1

day 1

control

day 3

day 3

control

light stick insects on dark leaves

stick insects go dark

Glossary

Abdomen
The part of an insect's body behind the third pair of legs. It contains the digestive organs, the sex organs, fat stores and much of the breathing system.

Camouflage
The way in which an insect's body is colored or shaped so that it is not noticed by its enemies.

Chitin
The substance that covers an insect's body.

Chrysalis
The name given to the pupa of a butterfly or moth.

Honeydew
A sugary substance produced by greenflies and similar insects which feed entirely on plant juices.

Labium
The "lower lip" section of an insect's mouthparts.

Labrum
The "upper lip" section of an insect's mouthparts.

Larva
The feeding and growing stage in the lives of many insects.

▽ Many insects have developed special methods for protecting themselves against their enemies. For example, the eyed hawk moth (left) looks like a piece of bark. If a bird attacks it, it draws aside its forewing to display realistic eye-marks. The pussmoth caterpillar (below) scares birds with its strange, face-like appearance and the waving tails at its rear end.

Mandibles
The chief cutting and chewing parts of an insect's jaws.

Maxillae
The second pair of "jaws" in an insect's mouthparts. They help to push food cut by the mandibles into the mouth.

Nectar
A sugar solution produced by flowers on which many insects feed.

Nymph
A term used for the young stages of some insects which do not go through full larval and pupal stages. Nymphs look rather like their parents, although their wings are not fully developed until they have grown and molted to their adult form.

Pupa
The non-feeding stage in the life of many insects, during which they change from their larval form to the adult shape.

Scavenger
An animal that feeds on dead plant or animal remains.

Thorax
The central part of an insect's body, between the head and the abdomen. It carries three pairs of legs and two pairs of wings.

Veins
Fine tubes which act as the supporting framework for an insect's wings. They contain air and nerves and some colorless blood. The wings of insects that have a nymph stage usually have a complicated network of veins. Those that have a larval stage have a simple network.

ant nest

bee nest

▽ Almost all insects live for themselves alone, but a few kinds live in colonies. Ants live in untidy nests, but they can react to an enemy attack by moving their eggs or grubs to another part of the nest. Termite nests are often huge mounds. They are sometimes so hard that they can only be broken into with a strong axe. Bumble bees live in small colonies, but other bees live in huge groups in nests made largely of wax. Wasps make their nests of paper formed by chewing scraps of wood.

termite nest

wasp nest

31

Index